Feeling All the Kills

T0338845

Feeling All the Kills

Helen Calcutt

First published 2024 by
Liverpool University Press
4 Cambridge Street
Liverpool
L69 7ZU

British Library Cataloguing-in-Publication data
A British Library CIP record is available

ISBN 978-1-80207-472-7 softback

Typeset by lexisbooks.com, Derby
Printed and bound in Poland by Booksfactory.co.uk

'poems
she gives them up.
they burn
jewels into jewels.'

Lucille Clifton, *fury*

Contents

Venus de Milo speaks

My nudity bears these effects of light.
Still, I am missing pieces of flesh.
Beyond any restoration
and so, in your eyes

difficult.
A whole range of new positions
for you to fuck me in
have been suggested.

Leaning slightly forwards
against a wall.
Resting my forehead on the floor.
Holding your belt

in my mouth,
as you get into it.
Either way, I define
the 'classical woman' for you.

A quiet one's air
of aloofness. Tried,
now passive, with this
hairstyle and marbling of flesh;

it evokes the very kind of woman
likely to stand before a kitchen sink
and get fucked on, slowly.
Do you imagine me holding

an amphora, or bow?
I could be Artemis, or a Danaid,
though you presume I'm the goddess of love
such is my half-nakedness,

these almond curves.
Perhaps once I lifted a silvered
urn. A teacup? Book?
Apple? Crown?

Whatever you think of
is whatever I am willing to hold,
invisibly –
and you can come at me

in all the ways you want.
Just don't reach for my hands,
never seen or touched.
A touch of mine, never felt.

Poem

When at last you withdrew,
the light lowered in my chest.
Gas lamp, in a field of poppies.

It's been confusing each time,
telling you (in my head) 'this
is how plant life survives

in a warzone'.
In the crossfire between
a man's search

of an entry wound
for his entry wound,
I did.

I was the red you see
in all those paintings
of shadowy men

standing over something quiet,
quietly.

— — — —

Most days I feel a mourning slowness,
like my knees and thighs are relics.

I wash, dress,
make my daughter breakfast.

She sings as I stare
at the illegible sky – all that ache,

the little holes of light
falling through us.

The doom reserved for enemies
marches on the ones we love …

It's the oldest kind.
To be held by your traumas.

Even as you bathe,
sex,

kiss,
pick little socks up off the floor.

I wash our cups. The knives.
She goes to school

I do the bedrooms,
the beds.

I,
lie down

and touch myself,
handfuls,   quickly

lifting a fine bronze urn.
How to say,

I lie back
and feel a scythe passing into me.

How to talk about _ _ _ _?
Feeling it now, as it was,

so many hands.
Many fingers and tongues

fisting you.
Do you deny this, yes or no?

I am an artifact.
I wash the dishes

I fuck
I remember, how,

when dying under him
I smelt the blood.

After 'the sex',
He didn't ask –

and he knows this,
I know this.

Know this:

I alone see what I suffer now.

Lines in italics from *Antigone* by Sophocles.

He saw them as I did

pausing to admire the incredible lilacs.

I can't reconcile,
one from the other.

How   to have me there
over all that mangled brass?

How   at the same time
to purr under a nodding flower?

*

They say purple is the colour
of the soul realising
her scope

for understanding.

Thick-set, summer dusk when it tilts.

how wonderful the man,

how awful

how wonderful   how awful

and so on—

I get it.

But I shouldn't.

Accountability often dies this way
(men die any other way possible).

Going underground

I have stood among them
and pitied.
I pity myself.

We, who are rocked together
and like many in this womb
want for love –

at this feeling edge,
coiled for breath, a herd
of breathless passengers

as the dark against us squeals.

*

We comfort ourselves.
Books, phones,
music,

'the stare' –
and when we alight
it's barely a memory.

Though I touched the shoulder
of one. Maybe his hand
too, as if

we haven't swayed
together?
We made our way

from one level to the next,
entirely alone.
Like Eve or Adam

we journeyed and ended
intending, perhaps,
to be naked

*

And when I'm home
and my baby is resting
in my arms – I hear.

When I close my eyes, fumbling at my dress,
loosening the buttons and
tumbling my breast

as she suckles and suckles
and suckles to rest

I hear

*

We made love once

I blanked it out –
as you entered me,

as it happened.

There was the woodcutter's blade in the tree.

My eyes were white
under hundreds and hundreds of
deliberate strokes.

A crow

burned far off

and a train, farther still, screamed
with a dog at its heels –

(or a woman who is a dog
who would give anything to be healed).

In so many terms

Abduction. I say it out loud.
'Something or someone taken'
I'm a mad woman with cats except
I talk to things, giving them names.

Maltreatment. A bag scuffs the curb,
as if it wants to touch.
A man across the street, watches
blows into his hands.

Molestation.
The syllables go down well.
It feels good to say, *violation,*
depredation, despoilment,

these sweet wrappers, three,
pillageplunder down the street (the man
blowing into his hands
walks away).

Rapine. I look into someone's
house, and imagine if it were mine.
The light, my bones.
The interior,

my emotional property.
A leaf touches my ankle,
a thigh,
a sigh as it goes.

The trees

What binds them is their hair.
Roughed against headboards,
twitching.

Their eyes globe wide
it's through me, and beyond.
I ask, "who,

or what,
victimised your roots?"
Soft overwhelm

suddenly remembering.
They know,
I know,

disgrace like this.
The embarrassment of their leaves
on and around each other

is a mad, mad mutter.
I understand what they say.

Feeling all the kills

Nothing at first.
Not even the three-inch needle
they sink into your spine.
You imagine its splitting ends
and flickerings. Like a city
burning into white noise,
then blackout.
How often do you have ten
men working on you?
Going down on you
in the raw places.
Filling the gaps
between their fingers
with your blowsy dust,
they lift you, then,
your legs—open you whole
for two halves.
How exposed is your belly?
Buttocks? Vagina?
And the soul? It floats,
like a blade beneath global lights
and you watch it, thinking
if it can glisten that way –
in this place, so can I …
with so much movement happening
above you,
so many blue-winged coats.
And you, a sterile, sack of meat.
You can't be human
in a place like this.
Every time you lift your head
to vomit, someone appears

to catch it, wipe it clean.
Still, you want to feel safety
of a kind, the true cold
of the bars as you
hold them.
Just as you would your keys
phone, purse – everything
is like the everyday,
except you could die on this one.
Strangers unknotting
an arm-length inside of you.
Dragging out
the rotting plate,
those surgeons of cherubim,
and that exquisite music from the radio on air –
you could just
peel away, like the first
embryonic you conceived,
though you have lived these 32 years
you could give up—just
bleed and bleed and bleed
the stuck fuse, the second
sack-worm of essential life
that kept your child
alive, but somehow,
is murdering you.
And you're witnessing it all
as you lie there.
Whatever cut or crushed,
envelopes the viscous sack
as they slacken it. Whoever
devalued or debased,
humiliated, scorned,
rent – like two halves of a nervous flower
– and stuffed you.

You take each with a gulp
of air, a cup of water,
as you are shelled,
sucked on, cleaned.
You accept, full-boned
this cleansing touch.
The drop of sweat on the brow
is a holy kiss, it might
melt and blur you to nothing.
But your guardian
is gliding,
gliding.
You're rising
with the riding beats
of your heart—
each one,
each one,
though they say,
'the blood loss is extensive'
and start to stitch.
And how often do
you get to be the one
who does this?
At once, opened and purged
over a sparkling table.
At once, feeling all the kills.

Placenta moment

The way this bag clings to the branch like a womb
sack,

and the river flows one way,
like afterbirth, and the tip of the branch
is heavy with sludge,
as if two hands
had parted the parts of a girl.
Numbed, tugging at the rubied insides.

The way I thought my blood moved through me
like chains, now I see, is a river.
And because it nearly killed me
I never saw the placental form.
Grim, this putrid one
nudged by the river like the surgeon's
spade, the arm, which slipped so
easily into my cunt and
worked at it,
worked at it.

It felt like the dogging
does — this nodding river. Rising to reach
this sluice, this heavy, falling
in uneven halves
little shelled out moons,
what once was good to the earth.

And this flimsy plastic bag ... well
it must be my soul, the mere
glassy-eyed shade of it.
Humble as the light in it,
clinging on,
thinking it is about to die.

Middle of the night moment

Feeling my way to my daughter's bed.
Her mole-dark head,
and those eyes

I thought would be closed in sleep
are open, and there's singing.
These weeding hours

I unfurl myself.
Leaf,
by skin,

touch, and slip,
a golden file
into the pages of dawn.

Tending to her, then
trying to write 'that line' about
the night I was –

the moment I –
it could have been my hands were tied?
But they weren't,

and I sort of smiled
as I opened my legs to him anyway.
You have to give in like that.

Backwards, or forwards
it makes no difference, either way
your eyes, your mind

are delivered into confusing beauty.
Seeing it all, and trying to make it
happen differently.

I nearly lose myself, but
who would I be without it?
What would I say?

Once

and only once,

an owl

levelled its life across my life.

Lifting me where it dropped
exactly to the moment
where snow-light collapsed

then reformed,

brushing a wing over my eyes.

I was seeing my self
touched. My sight,
snow-touching.

Lifting across years into an echo
of rooms,
where starkly, we two

stood
wing-bound under a light,
nakedly trusting

in a moment that would bind.
Touched, as I had been once before
but only as a child. Gently.

Returning

Last night,
the snow lay down its gift upon the world.

When people woke, they saw
and forgetting the laws

of *thou shalt not*, stepped out
into unbiblical whiteness.

They disarmed their yards
of gagging cloth. Undressing,

as they walked through the trees
to the tops of hills,

the little slopes and valleys.
They stood and surveyed the effortless,

the wild. They looked on the snow
and she on them,

turning their faces to each other
in the pale light— making sounds like

laughter, love, free talk.
Their voices, as if attached by thread,

kited. Gathering in all lightness and height
to shape the air: a bell dropped in stillness.

Then tremors, the tentative
utterance of thought: *shall we go down,*

this way?
All the way,

together?
glimmering and revealing

in the un-swaddling air,
a chorus of relief.

Their hands were so raw and cold,
but it felt glorious –

and the snow-faith
clinging to the trees, whispered

so they remembered,
through the falling edges

and dust-halves of their souls
play, and *touch*. Recalled

the gnawing chasms
of well-earned hunger.

And the more this took over,
the more they dazzled –

like ruddy prisms in the light.
Winter haze was a darling lover

returning to greet them,
embracing their children first, as she should

lifting them to ascend, like tropical birds,
many-coloured over this marbling earth.

And then, the adults too,
opened their human wings. Flew.

For Daphne unborn

My tongue takes your life for medicine
and I pray you are well, for the swell
of your damaged heart.

I've been staring at the bluebells
too long. Drowsy,
under their skirts and skins,

mouthing 'chime' and 'clink',
seeking clarity.
Just as birds may chitter,

blue-throated in the dark.
As we hear them from our beds
treading under our hearts, such a call,

is a signal through the curtain
and our only way through.
Oh, its persistence is charm.

Even when doubt flays the mind
with brute rain, I hear it,
in my own listening faith

down the tender, tilting path.
Faint, yet effortless
and gaining with time.

Just a little more time.

Josephene speaking about
her unborn sister

She told me

life,
will pour straight in, if you let it

if you draw back the curtain   just enough,
let her small head
her body   like the shadow of a horse
pass,   press   through the glass, even
collecting you and your grief
with it.

She told me

her sister is a horse
because she holds the scent of earth,
the bind of mud.
That impressions   of a hoof
stonewarm   are what I want,

a body on a body,
a baby-holding love.

All this

without expectation or return.

All this

from an old-handed sun,

through this vertical continuum,
an opening yes,

moving forwards, yes

forgiveness in the form of a daughter, yes.

We three

Never happier than this.
The sigh of morning has us,
breath of our breath

in the exhale.
The bedsheet is pale
as the mist, disrobing in folds,

collecting again in smoke
to cup the air, still warm.
The safety of your head

is a crown.
You, my eldest,
have slept with me

since you were one day old.
My youngest snores.
Steady as paws across hard-earthed

snow, where pages fall,
and I lean in to write.
It's the clarity of the three of us.

I have to wake you,
but I want to make words,
watch you sleep.

Sheep-skin warm, and disappearing,
a leafy stir, then bones;
bones and sheets collecting,

a new sigh, *I am safe here*
a small dream
beginning.

I want you to go on, and on.
Stride weightless and beautiful
into that private world,

and let me have no part in it
but to witness this cocoon
of female wonder.

Your sister,
you,
and I.

To be your mother here,
next to you,
near to her.

And never for a moment need
anything other than
this.

All at once

the buddleia was raided by butterflies.
Lolling tongues too thick for their mouths

fell whispers. Confined at first
to the low walls of the garden, then

permanent flickerings around the head.
They knew what they wanted to happen.

That it would be difficult,
but I was so sick and so ready for it—

they entered and exited my body
in exactly the same way. Tiny wings

tapped hard, the ring-knot fuse
hot as screams, and the room gleamed

six inches deep in bloodwater.
Souped with placenta, thick as a neck.

Fierce the images,
but formed,

formed.
In the crackling distance

between 'I and the tree',
that closed, when they seeded and grew.

The 'I and them' (oh the miles)
that appeared

when they met oxygen – drank
the scaly, cardinal textures of

mood,

       mother,

father: *"bad dynamics."*

Their feet became their own too quickly.
It took them twenty years down the road together

before they'd even left me.
Swaying quiet hips. Burning hair and lips.

'No'

They show me what it means
to disrupt the flow
of my absolute desire
to hold them.

And I didn't realise
daughters could resist
the touch of their mother,
but they do,

and it's clear.
The slight fingers and palms
that lift, quickly, from the centreline
of a sailing body

push, and I am away.
I resist, perhaps
a moment, a second.
But then realise,

and realise again –
that when they anchor love
with their eyes,
but moor the space with their hands

they have grown to see
their soft selves
as solo islands
to remain islands.

And they have a right.

Disturbance

has leaked through many times
discovered it can make music.
The blow of a hand

to a head, for instance.
What might have been a puppeting
mouth, played heavy before the quiet,

the pale keys, the dark.
What they heard,
you saw (I am speaking

to my wardrobe).
You have two holes
a key or tooth might unpick.

Much like these holes
above my hips,
where the wings split.

I wasn't trying to fly.
I can't remember
how the rest of him touched me,

if my eyes were closed.
When I stop to think, I see her face,
though I hardly remember the room.

If she was there at all.
If she covered her face with her hands,
or glowed, like a moon.

You held on

smoke lurched to fire,
they kept pouring on leaves.

All around, the candelabras of light
were beginning to rage.

We witnessed so many going up –
their purpled limbs dismembering,

casting wide over hoodless trees
who leaned in, and observed us.

We, mother and child,
were in the only stillness we knew.

Men were building fires with dirt.
Piling bodies over wood,

lighting arrows,
sending them up.

I kissed your head – *it'll be alright*,
but something fell behind your eyes

and you unmoored.
Later, you slept.

I washed the milk bottles,
put them out.

I saw the whole,
blown open chasm of rage.

Locks on a cage—
shattered jaw, steaming paths.

And beneath me still, the sinking ground.

Listen

there's the instep of the moth,

its terrible tribe of ancestors.

Ancestors of wingbeats
that are wings,
burning, fluttering hands.

Life is beautiful and damaging enough.
Life is dazzling and damaging enough.

Why does the moth never stop?

Bath time

Knowing I have to leave,

knowing this,

is what keeps me here.
Ornament and subject to your keen advances,
your careful taps.

You want to see if I'm still alive.
I bloom when our daughter touches me,
but when you …

my skin draws a pallid glaze
and I want to hold
and hold

another innocence of feeling.
I don't want to be seen in any other way.
I'll keep on making the pure things,

the sweet-blood, growing things.
Be still, like pottery,
let the green stems grow,

the vessel or charm
you want to nibble on, suck.
Lie smooth and round,

depressed in the bath.
Let the water come over me, like fakery
in sex, and like all those other times—

lie back, and listen for hope in the rain.
Stare hard, like those trees
with their hair thrown forwards.

I've learned to feel their downward ache.
I know what kind of life that is,
sustaining a fall.
Barely alive, barely breathing.

Wonderful

Over the years they've climbed
to the very lip of the sash,
her fingerprints.
And where she's knelt,
bowing upwards, a golden reed,
the marks have scattered
a constellation of effort;
the hours, days, weeks,
of learning how to grow.
She loops her fingers
around my thumb,
my heart unlocks.
You see,
it's that she's touching
me, and whenever
someone touches me
(especially her)
I want to cry.
I want to tell her
I love her.
But instead, I say
Mommy's sad today.
She slips from the bed
to the floor, walks
to her little stool:
opens the window.

It will take years

for this spider
to get from one side of the door
to the other.
Lowering herself
in sinewy dimensions, between
something like exhaustion and grace,
from the wall to the white borders

it has taken
all the love of her body
to open over the wood.
Tip-toeing
as you might across
water or ice,
lifting and lowering,
dipping and
realigning.
Kissing her own threads.

Everything is done
so deliberately, and with such
innocence. The weariness
of her spider-body
makes me want to loop
my hands,
hold her near to my heart
– beating as it does,
for something keen
to start in it.

But foot-stooled beside
my daughter's bed,
I only watch.

And then
wonder, how long it will take
this spider to crawl
from her noon-dark interior,
across this chasm of no return
into the daylight.

The hour of holding

It's always the same.
I am away, and I can feel it.
I am with him, but watching the sky
and wanting to know
how it looks to your eyes
as they observe the blanket fall,
and the heavy moves through you.

Someone else strokes the grain
of curtains as they're closed.
I'm in a hotel, or on a beach.
The waves are bending far back –
such mothers,
in this hour of holding.
Their hair cascading

down the spine of the black.
They take the weight of bringing
a somewhere-child
into them.
I brought you into me.
Now the light that held me in its eyes,
is adrift. I am cordless,

on pebbles and sand, these
round, cold hours are the ones
before something breaks,
tilts, and I see
mothers with their daughters,
going home.

Their footsteps, one-two,
over the little dunes.
Tenuous paths.

Last time, I said
I would be doing this with you.

Refugee mother

for the mothers rescued by Mo Chara,
who lost their babies to the sea

I deserve no more
than to be rolled
from the hip of the sea.
To crawl like a dog
on the wet sand.
Made to stand,
when the world
is a cracked jug
pouring daylight.
Strangers
washing me with salt,
asking
is that your baby
floating
on the wing of a shawl?
My clothing
everywhere, and then
my blood. Other women,
crackling like moons,
their mouths tinning
a racket of spoons—
And if they asked me
What was her
name?
Where are you
from?
Do you have ten
minutes
to declare

you're vulnerable?
I would think of her
hands,
that they're pretty.
One summer
they unfolded a
wish in
my belly.
My breasts would hang
like globes. I'd feel their pull.
They'd hang like
wet doves
bleeding milk.

And now your voice comes saying

"Can I walk alone?"
Our path is making its journey to the sea,
the leaves that line the curb

are a waterfall.
I'm aware
of your hand in mine.

The wick strands of your hair
are bright and miraculous as this container
of air—the bigness of the road.

Your hand slips.
The spaces between our fingers
fall to salt and grass.

The sky portal is burning
her last phoenix.
Three years ago, you tricked death.

The green old gate, to the bus stop
(where we eat oranges)
is a watercolour transcending

its fine-boned tissue paper.
I've never asked how it is
you managed to make your way.

Because then I'll know.

Crayon

Bless these pieces,
these two.
Not ruby or apple
but the cleft inner wound of a peach,
two parts the same flesh.

And I wonder for a moment,
if I ate such a fruit.
If anything I touched (including
you) or our daughter's box
of artist's jewels,

bled over with the same colour?
She holds aloft the little crayon.
As if God himself
had split adrift its halves
once seeming so belonging,

now resting, like two in a bed,
untouching.

And she's just asking and asking and
asking and asking,

Can you fix it Mommy? Can you fix it?

I can't go any further

I get stuck
on 'the backs of his knees
like Mayagi oysters'.
So, I'll begin

on the floor again, fucked.
The spaces in my head
are ticking round. The tips
of my nipples are hard,

darker than before.
My shoulders are sloping like
Venus de Milo's.
I nearly glow,

but I'm on mute. My hands
don't tremble if I clasp them
but if I let go,
there, see?

They're uncontrollable.
Something or someone
murmurs, 'get up'.
I can't stop looking at my hair—

so fucked up and wild.
There are two
horns pulsing out
from under my head,

my mouth looks so
red,
eyes – alien as ink,
with the pupils spilling over.

I vomit,
and it's milky, fish-bits.
In the mirror
there's a girl.

Now a woman.
A girl,
somehow, a woman.
And we gaze outwards

through this prism of
untellable
self-refraction
and

Bringing the washing in

I carry the bodies of cotton.
One by one, give their innocence to the air.
I show the world how casual I can be
whilst doing it. Hanging them
corner to corner by thread.
Little doused skins, wrinkled hearts.
When I'm done, I lie upstairs in my room.
I sleep and wake to the moans of the house,
the creaks in the loft, the limes
groaning and lurching softly.
I hear my clothes being slapped
on the line. The sky throws dark occasionally—
and I feel a surge of love,
knowing they're defenceless.
The air is pinning them so high—
their reds and blues,
sapphires, whites – might
rip, struggle (but not
struggle) and fly.
I lie here, waiting for it to happen.
It's just clouds from my window
for so long. Then the wind,
collapsing her jaws over the roof.
The sky bowling wet euphoria.
All that fury that has been coming
finally does. I run,
cradling my head like a victim,
and quickly, softly,
urgently, fervently,
pull my gentlings from the line.
Sun and rain are hurtling their arrows,
as I hold and hold these slips from my soul

and the feeling is better than sex.
It opens like sex, on a warm day
and holds me like a mother's breast.
The satisfaction, is like milk.
These garbs, my lambs,
have me right here,
where I need to be,
as I gather them in,
and cry a little, whisper,
I can't let you go.

Poem for my hips

Hold me, then let go.
Pull backwards, slowly
so it's just my hips floating.

Allow me this.
To be a part, yet distinct

as if a ball of light were circling

and I were open to

rage,
orgasms,
light –

and could experience them all
at the same time.

I won't stop if you pull back.

From here, these hips
they might even smile,

sink down onto our bed,

ask for this again.

Pale deer, soft-footed

The water is silk. She sings to me.
The cold wind, the streets, the people
flicker and shut off when the water
falls, and I am naked within.

Singing of my dirt, how to know it.
My eyes close … in these sacred moments
when my daughters sleep and my loved
one reads about Vikings, and flayed skin.

The water is like a pattering of milk.
I want to stoop, and lick, and taste life again—
I ask, *did I give too easily today? Was I good?*
baring my throat to the sky, the lit tiles

reflect a deer, pale, soft-footed.
I run my fingers down my hair
in St Water. I pray to her, *choose me*
flow over, and over, and over me,

touch me, heal.

Heal, until I am no longer meek or mild
and I can run with my sins again.

As quickly as your seeing lowers

drawing back on the bow, which unlets,
like your hands as they undress me
beautiful with feeling.
You need me.
But to say this would
prove yourself keen
and falling,
you're so … you say, *I like this …*
as I turn and drop
the loosened thread,
I become Swan, your room
a blackish lake I surface onto
that you witness, and
for half a second,
drown inside.
You fall asleep behind
and around.
I can't, so I watch
that seeing part of you
scatter over my eyes onto the window
which for some reason,
you keep open.
In the morning I hear grass-heads singing.
You're still here.

'So many things, so many
things in on you'

under the Moroccan lantern.
Between Libya, and Birmingham.
All those other women tickering on loop,

then I –
the little rounded stoop.
I carry myself well

but you see,
where there might have been wings
instead, plays a mothy darkness.

You told me you could hold
my whole waist with just
one hand. I felt your hard

heart beating. There were bars
from which I stared behind,
but when you moved inside

I fell open, like a forest.
I climbed my way between
the search of your hands

and loved that your eyes
were like sparrow-mouths
closing, opening,

closing, opening.
'Fuck', you said.
I didn't want to be screwed on so

tight—but when you pressed my feet
onto your thighs,

and hammocked the tandem of my

hips – my purpose fluttered.
'It's happening,' I muttered.
The spaces under my shoulders began to lift.

In spite of this

We drove through the mist as if flying.
Home was a speck on the horizon,
and for moments at a time
the fields held my heart.
Wetted bladeish through sunrise,
we sped over roads. I felt the hollow way
into a wood enter, my love's jewel,
melted and expanded in the ribs of grass,
suffocated too, and together
we lighted and spoored, became
almost nothings in the sways
of your deliberate quietness.
You were far and armoured as the frost.
As bleak, sudden, as the owl
I only imagined falling;
gifting wide and white above our heads,
to thread our voices—*look, how beautiful!*
hoping to break the iron that held us
fast, for reasons I will never
(as always) truly understand.
But then I do.
I love you, and I love you in ways
you can't fathom or accept.
And you love me in spite of this.

We pray differently

And so, we've arrived.
The trees and sky are a moving tapestry
stirring like strings.
At once, cloud and light,
at last, soft in agreement.
By fingers. By unfamiliar
warmth, we're tied.
Cut from very different cloth,
our silks and shirks, never belonging.
Now here, where a breezy love,
an effortless, has entered.
Terrifying, isn't it?
Our ears and eyes are new to this.
You shine with all the brilliance
of darkness rolled
between hands.
I am all auburn and fire, an oil-panting.
Cresting the hue of any credible
grudge – to seek a bronzing balance,
collecting each, in the golden arms of the other,
holding the weight of the other,
as we do ourselves.
I am happy to say,
my heart has already bled its strings
for this. We vowed, and so did.
Patterned as velvet with the moving chords,
the curious tug and thread of
what I call God,
what you call God.
Yes, we pray differently.
Your palms may kiss the earth,

my feet may wander it.
Still, we're bowed.
Palm to sole. Lit.

Shelling the beans

He showed me how.
With hands I'd never seen before,
movements, never witnessed.

I squatted low, as he came in
around me.
His arms were like

my brother's arms, open as an oak.
Chest, a breathing barrel.
This is a good man,

I thought,
and haloed through his catching.
I craned towards

his shining load.
Full, with moon-eyed grains.
This is what we need you to be,

he said,
but I misheard.
It was the beans speaking,

lucid and smooth,
pulsed, witting.
They explained:

you have to take away
our skins.
It's like opening

the velvet of your own
flaws,
it's something

you have to want
to do.
I did.

He lowered a sheath
into my palm,
and from the nib

of its uppermost eye,
pulled downwards.
They fell away more

effortlessly
than I could have imagined.

*

Later I realised,
I admired their willingness
to fall.

How twilight
touched them blue,
unarmoured.

Going slow

The way scent enters a room,
or two fingers press
the seat of a spine.

Lifting clothes after rain.
The skin might be plain
beneath, but it's the way

a person moves,
the way it makes you want to.
I can only do this

by exiting. Falling,
into a blind spot under your ribs,
consenting the moment as it happens

elsewhere (the tip of
every tiny hair?)
I am making wide

a senseless web.
Fluttering, like moon heads
over a private dock.

Just as lust in me is a ghost
want, and wanting too,
defer – bring the shadowed host.

A beautiful thing

I

How do we walk through to God?
That humble place, where the last voice you hear
is in the sun,

all tenderness and experience exhaling.
I believe the very moment you die from
is the moment you long for

all your life.
No expectation,
no expectation, at last.

The heat can fade away.
The heavy limbs
willow into epitaph

blackish free,
breath, whitish pollen.
And what is a human

if only halftone?
All the colours and candour of life,
second-veiled,

a vessel, for whatever entered you
that you endured,
with your back towards the sun's grate,

all tenderness and experience exhaling.
What is a person, if only this?
No feeling,

no feeling at last.
The old masks fading away

upturned, leaving every asking breath

un-paining into wide,
into ocean-wide clear,

apathetic light.

II

Something moves outside.

I could touch it?
Only if I become something else,
and drift – a kind of spontaneous dust

through the darkened glass
to the other side.

I want to let, *the soft animal of my body*
love what it loves,
which is a kind of death.

I accept, willing
yet, unfeeling almost.
Mute as a low-gold, living room light,

and allow,
allow,
allow …

… falling into you this way means,
I am smiling.
You're here, in this poem.

The glass has lifted
like a childhood curse.

You hold my face in your hands

and kiss it
once, twice, three times,
like mother to child.

I have become
my own hands holding.
My own eyes seeing

what strange and curious
newness,
what beauty.

* Sentences in italics from 'Wild Geese', by Mary Oliver.

Ash

As if thunder had decided against itself
and become woman
(not man – all hammer and tongues).

Spreading herself over the wide, gazing up.
Like a sheet you pull over the dead
except life,

life, is pulsing.
Any desire …
has drowned in the drift

of her purpose,
which I can't grasp.
So I settle inside her

like a rounded sleep.
Her gaze, as it falls, weightless.
My stammers,

darting on mute terms
between soft grades of sunlight,
evening clementine.

So much I could say, but
can't,
in this

ash/snow
ash (as she is) and
putting her ear to my lips

at the same time
scatters, not wanting to know.
As if 'want' could occur

in many fractions of ways,
in many fractions
of a second.

As if I could feel held
by simply being present,
even when no comfort comes.

I stay with the snow
her steady burn,
saying and seeking nothing.

Who is Crow?

First shadow on the bridge before marriage.
The mask on the counter,
in my hands for a moment.
I forget her, then it's a face
I see over and over.
She blew clumsily, then composed
two scratches on the brick,
rick-rick.
Split her feathers
as you might a ribcage—
cawed – 'I can't breathe',
stamped her feet as if wanting
to murder something.
I know her fire.
I'm often alone on the couch
and the chimney is expunging
feather-mad – the black
hems and halters
I must have dismantled in my sleep.
What if I said, yes?
The fakery of it.
Some nights, it's all the birds
in the chimney un-guttering.
On others, it's only a small sound.
A tapping on the chest,
the cove of my ear,
nagging, nagging.
I pass her bridge
in my dreams and daily.
I've never seen her as I did
that night – knuckle-splayed,
and such a crown.

When I asked her if she would guide me
out of my sleepwalk,
what happened next—
was that her whole body freed itself.
Bolted diamond
over the vines of water,
that shuddered to take her in.

Moher Wild, crest by crest

I understand it here.
The way mist is not itself, until the rock
and rock is not rock, until the sea.

But if I step, crest by crest,
across these waters
there'll be no return.

Even if you, my abridged
token of luck, were a mark (ever-fixed)
on the gullwhite lines,

and you waved …
no matter.
My feet would be lifting with salt,

my lips, with astral air – its assemblance
of stars,
of scars,

DNA fibres,
and ancestral relapse.
I couldn't speak

of how bravely we've loved.
I'd be lost – as would you
to a *birth-right ephemera*.

Realising,
the meaning of 'home'
is belonging nowhere and to no one.

Mother, the city

for Birmingham

When the train pulls in, and I rise,
she folds onto her knees,
bows her blue-scarfed head.
The back of her neck is long, swanlike.
She reveals her scars like no other city.
And if her body is breaking this way?
The ribcage unpetaling; bone, by flimsy bone,
then she has floated alight
to observe such a break.
Such a selfless, slow way to suffer.
She hangs, like speech marks
with nothing to say.
And all the while there is movement below,
there is us – touching, bleeding, killing, kindling –
and above and between, our dying witness, sees all.
Asks (with an effort to stand) 'how to mend?'
reaching, to touch, what?
Our hands, our hearts,
our incorrigible lips?
I tell you, she has come on all fours
from traumatised air – from our own *mouths*.
Spirited with so much darkness,
yet so much contradiction to that dark.
And on into dawn, her tiny miracles unseen.
While the quiet heave of her mothersome sphere
gathers our sighs as they're orphaned,
whispering, 'oh, what can I do?'
spreading her hands upon us all,
as we try to feel her.

A song in Highbury Park

We heard him first.
She stood, and listened.
I watched, like a guard

with the halved sun
gilding her image and mine.
She was new to the sound of it.

Such moany-cries
through the goosy neck.
He worked sick –

to give more and more of
(what I presumed to be)
every tragic and

unresolved part of him.
She asked me,
"Why?"

Then laughed.
It made no sense,
but it was right and complex

that she wanted to touch
his sleeves.
That she danced

to his ridiculous music,
somewhat afraid.
She giggled when he dropped

the pipes from his lips,
and smiled at her.
It was right, and complex,

that she looked to me
for permission to smile
back. That I allowed it.

Dark Sun

Maybe I don't know what it means to be raped.
I wasn't blindfold
(I was)

we agreed on things
(we didn't).
I was on all fours, then

flat as a lily.
I saw myself thinking
I would be loved

differently as he went
down there.
Stapled something together,

then unstapled it.
It was like a stun-gun up the raw
end of my rubicund

anus.
There were sounds
like a drill. The spiralled nail.

Ever-so, inch by inch.
A surprise,
and fucking nasty.

Sperm-hairs curled thinly.
I wanted to put my hands
there – he hated that.

He said,
be

many things,

scatter
yourself,

and I tried,
as blood pooled a sun.
I heaved my birdish chest, my

sep - a - ra - ting
toes, fingers,
to grasp. Let loose.

I think I failed.

Summer Solstice

Who left out the dropsy?
The long-sleeved
cream satin and lace.
Their ends, cow-tongued,
saying this thing,
that thing.

All whispers in the solstice.
The sun loosened her straps
removed her dress,
and lay down
(it will be until midnight).

Until that dark sky within us
notices the dark sky.
Until we feel the heaviness of roads,
the ones we lie upon
(so hot out here)

and the ones we don't.
Until that woman you saw,
who could have been you
looks back, and signals,
'that's it, it's finally over.'
Until then.

You can hear a train coming

and when the track starts to burn—
the ones inside yourself
here, held fast
and close to the ground.

Let your mind walk here.
Drop to your knees between platforms
and with your ear to the bar,
listen
for the kennel of dogs, and don't move.

'Burn, jewels into jewels'

I am trying very hard
to undress.
The slack of a gown
keeps leaving me, almost.
But in this moment of disrobing
it stays, and I am standing here,
wanting him to remove it.
My neck is long as a train track.
And he is going in to kiss it
there – on the right side.
The warmth mouth,
familiar as peach,
but it's not happening.
People are coming and going
interrupting us, however,
I do trust him to do this,
because in the pit of me –
he is already doing this.
If I can just navigate
his mouth, his hands, as if
they were my mouth, my hands,
I can bring this all into me.
I'll have a way of making him work
that won't need or sob
for milk – but will move
a quick light inside of me.
Between my gloved
thigh box, its slackened poles,
he will go. Curiously
and playfully into
and unfold – flip me on,
keen and steady at the base-wall.

It's the unveiling of a space
that is actually sacred.
I got on my knees
and swept the dirt out
long ago (as if there was ever
any there?) for my home
of personal chemistry, and magic.
Where the screaming goes,
when the screaming's done,
it glows up, gladly
stretched and fed.
Like tubes that make you live,
rather than stopping you die.
A single   'O'
rippling into many.
A girl-smile-child, a knowing
that love is present, and that I am.
It's all mine, even when I can't
properly dream it.
Reaching to bring
whatever surface of touch.
Scent of man,
dark hair eyes hands, barely
but absolutely would –
like to enter me, in daylight.
Because they do, all of them, ah.
A steady eye
is looking in here, it is
my reflection, and my joy that cascades now
unburdened—
because I want this,
and I'm announcing it too.
Into and unto and always.

Note from the poet: Seeking joy

I was in my late teens when I was assaulted, but I've only started talking about what happened to me in the last two years. I'm in my thirties now, and sadly, it's very common for women to begin their journeys of 'untangling' (untangling our fundamental identities from the shame of abuse) years after the event that caused it. Some of you reading *Feeling All the Kills* will also have suffered assault. If this is you, I whole-heartedly commend your courage to open these pages. It takes enormous strength of character to open the door back into a world your entire being will have fought hard for you to bury, and forget. 'Our pain pushes us to our vision.' I heard this on a podcast by Michael Beckwith, and this was the gamechanger for me. Following my joy, is now my habit. Feeling extreme pleasure, excitement, laughter; smelling the richness of the air, allowing my eyes to rest on the breathtakingly beautiful; allowing my ears to hear angelic qualities of the 'good things', like my daughters giggling, or a river babbling, or the 'ard nailed Brummie accent. Tuning into all that was, and letting it express itself fully in however it needed to – has left all this space for wonderful newness. It's scary, because it's unfamiliar. But it is mine.

Here is a list of resources, including direct charitable touchstones, to more creative explorations. Many of these tools helped me on my journey, I hope they might help you:

PANDAS Foundation (for mothers grappling with mental health concerns) www.pandasfoundation.org.uk

Rape Crisis England & Wales: www.rapecrisis.org.uk

SARSAS Charity: Support for people affected by rape or any kind of sexual assault or abuse at any time in their lives. www.sarsas.org.uk

Samaritans Charity (they have wonderful email service if phone conversations feel too much) www.samaritans.org

Detailed information on somatic therapies and how to get started: www.verywellmind.com/what-is-somatic-therapy-5190064

Healing Trauma: A Pioneering Program for Restoring the Wisdom of your Body by Peter Lavine. I also highly recommend his YouTube videos.

Living Magically by Gill Edwards

Healing Sex: A Mind-Body Approach to Healing Sexual Trauma, by Staci Haines

Acknowledgements

Thank you to the following publications where some of these poems, or previous versions of them, have appeared: *Poetry Wales, Poetry Ireland, The London Magazine, Oxford Brookes Poetry Centre, The High Window, Ink Sweat & Tears,* and *Irisi Magazine*. 'Mother, the city' was written for the Commonwealth Games Opening Ceremony, and lines from it appeared live on BBC1. Deep gratitude to the Society of Authors for awarding me a grant for works-in-progress, where many of these poems saw their beginnings. Thank you to Zoë Brigley Thompson for your wonderful poetic insight and endless support, and to Anthony Anaxagorou for your time, patience, and understanding. Deepest thanks to Deryn for creating a safe space in which to land these poems. The recognition alone that a duty of care, and careful editorial support was required here, was invaluable to the process of finishing this book. Thank you to Stuart Bartholmew and 'Somehow' (Verve Poetry Press) where a number of these poems first found their form. Sincere thanks also to my friend and poetry soul-mate Shaun Hill for 'seeing', supporting, and fully validating my identity as a woman and a poet. Finally, thank you to my parents for their openness to absolutely everything I set out to achieve. To my closest female friends who have allowed me to explore and identify my strengths in woman and motherhood. To Spike Barker for consistently supporting my space to work. And to my two golden daughters for their limitless inspiration.